Especially for

_____

From

_____

Date

_____

© 2006 by Barbour Publishing, Inc.

ISBN 978-1-61626-133-7

Compiled by Snapdragon Editorial Group.

All scripture quotations are taken from the King James Version of the Bible.

Published by Barbour Publishing, Inc., P.O. Box 719, Uhrichsville, Ohio 44683, www.barbourbooks.com

*Our mission is to publish and distribute inspirational products offering
exceptional value and biblical encouragement to the masses.*

Member of the
Evangelical Christian
Publishers Association

Printed in China.

365
Parenting
Secrets

BARBOUR
PUBLISHING

Train up a child in the way he should go:
and when he is old, he will not depart from it.

PROVERBS 22:6

When dealing with teenagers, keep in mind that you were young once. Your parents probably wondered about you from time to time, too.

New Year's Eve is a wonderful
time to set goals as a family.

Words to say daily: "Tell me more."
This encourages children to talk to you.

Set yearly goals with your children—things they would like to obtain, qualities they would like to develop, and skills they would like to acquire.

When packing a diaper bag, don't forget to include a disposable camera for those unexpected moments. They will happen when you least expect them.

No matter how ridiculous they seem,
respect your child's fears while working
together to find ways to overcome them.

Remember, being a good parent doesn't mean being perfect. It's a learning process that takes time.

In order for you children to have good friends,
they need to be good friends.
Explain how good friends treat each other.

Speak to your children with respect and courtesy. They deserve to be treated with the same consideration you would afford your friends.

Two things are critical to child rearing:
love and consistency!

January 7

Safety Tip: Never leave young children
unattended in the bath. They can slip and
go under in just a few inches of water.

You can talk to your children about making good choices, but they won't do so unless you give them the opportunity to try.

Family nights are wonderful ways
for families to connect. Schedule a weekly
night just for playing games and having fun.

December 25

Thou shalt conceive in thy womb, and bring forth a son, and shalt call his name JESUS.

LUKE 1:31

Always be prepared to answer the questions "Why?" and "Why not?" when you talk with your teenagers about values. This will help them understand that values have tangible benefits.

To create strong readers, create a book-rich environment. Place books in every room in the house. Let your children see you reading.

Give your children a list of their chores daily. It's a visual reminder that helps keep them on track.

January 9

Teach your children to serve others.
Volunteer at local nursing homes, homeless
shelters, or any place that reaches out to others.

Eat dinner at the same time whenever possible.
Eating together regularly can be a wonderful
source of family time and a perfect way to keep
a family in contact during a hectic week.

If you are constantly entertaining your children, they won't learn to entertain themselves.

Give your children your undivided attention
when they want to talk to you. It lets them
know you think they are important.

Children need to learn to do things simply
for the reward of helping others.
Provide unpaid opportunities to serve others.

Make a double batch of your favorite dishes.
Eat one and freeze the other. Use the frozen
one on those days when you would like to have
a little more time with your children.

Go Christmas caroling with friends, and encourage your children to share their voices with shut-ins and the elderly.

Rest is important when you have a new baby. Nap when the baby naps, put your feet up while feeding the baby, and go to bed early.

Teach children to tithe by giving them
a dollar's worth of dimes. They keep nine
dimes and put one in the offering.

The streets of the city shall be full of boys
and girls playing in the streets thereof.

ZECHARIAH 8:5

Reward charts are an excellent way to help young children reach goals. Have a reward all picked out and advertise it often with enthusiasm.

When dealing with behavioral problems, work with one or two problems at a time. Be patient; don't expect overnight results.

When one of your children is feeling overwhelmed with a task, help that child break it down into smaller, more manageable parts.

School-aged children do better in school when they eat well-balanced meals. Provide healthy lunches and avoid junk food and soda.

December 16

Being polite is never out of place.

Require your children to help with chores.
Even little ones can fold socks.
It teaches them responsibility.

When potty training toddlers,
use cloth underwear. Pull-up type
underwear feels just like diapers.

Got the winter blues? Have an indoor picnic! Spread blankets on the floor, make potato salad, and get out the squirt guns.

Scrapbook with your children. It doesn't have to be extravagant or fancy to be full of wonderful memories.

Open a savings account for each of
your children as soon as they get their first jobs.
Then teach them to put a portion of
their money away for the future.

Your influence over your children expires
when they become adults. Expose them
to important principles early and often.

Children need to believe they can succeed.
Encourage them to keep trying when they fail.
Confident children are more willing to try
something new and hang in there.

Plan a reward for you and your children when the family has a tough day to get through.

Teaching self-control is important. Children must understand that some behaviors are wrong. Expect them to behave appropriately.

Build self-confidence in your children daily.
Remember, confident children can
walk away from a bad situation more
easily then those who lack confidence.

Our children imitate what they see
us do and say. Set a good example that
your children will want to follow.

Role-play with your children about situations
they could encounter. Play "What if. . ."
and then discuss options to give
your children a game plan.

Provide a safe place for babies and toddlers to explore. They need room to crawl, play, and practice the new skills they are learning.

Encourage your children to make gifts
for the family this year. Homemade gifts
are especially appreciated by relatives.

Daughters need quality daddy time.
Dads, take your daughters on regular dates.

Encourage children to call or write relatives just to say hello. They shouldn't wait until they want something from Grandma or Grandpa.

Direct your children's activities,
but don't make unnecessary rules or try to direct
their every move. Let them be creative.

Give each child a special ornament
for the Christmas tree each year.
Then when they leave home, they will have
sentimental ornaments for their own trees.

Help young children learn to make decisions by giving them choices. Let them choose things like what shirt they will wear or what snack they will have before dinner.

Even preschoolers love competition.
Try playing "Who can pick up the most toys?"
or "Who can pick up their toys the fastest?"

Don't stop being watchful as children get older. Teens need guidelines and safety nets now more than ever.

Lay children's clothes out the night before for school or church. This helps to avoid the "What will I wear?" and "All my socks are in the washer!" problems in the morning.

January 29

Take time for yourself. You will be a better parent when you spend time taking care of you.

Words to say daily: "Let's pick up."
Children need order.

If your main baby-changing area is upstairs, keep a small basket stocked with extra diapers, lotion, and baby basics downstairs. This will save a few trips up and down the stairs.

Don't be afraid to let your children
decorate the Christmas tree. You can
have a perfect one when they are grown.

Write your children notes.
Saying "I love you" is important, and
notes are something they can save.

Focus on ways to give rather than receive this holiday season. Charity is a learned response.

Lo, children are an heritage of the LORD:
and the fruit of the womb is his reward.

PSALM 127:3

December 1

I have shewed you all things, how that so labouring ye ought to support the weak, and to remember the words of the Lord Jesus, how he said, It is more blessed to give than to receive.

ACTS 20:35

Teach your young children their names,
address, and phone number—important
but often overlooked facts.

Sing together. Music makes
any task more pleasant.

Words to say daily: "I believe in you."
It's a confidence builder.

Teenagers tend to be extremely loyal. Rather than telling them how much you dislike certain friends, focus on specific behaviors and ask for their perspective.

Make time alone with your husband a priority.
Schedule date night regularly—even if
it's in your own living room.

November 28

Use a timer to help children
finish chores on time.

Safety Tip: Place babies on their
backs when sleeping. This helps to prevent
Sudden Infant Death Syndrome.

Let a child take a favorite animal or toy with them when traveling. It will provide much-needed security in unfamiliar surroundings.

Let children help with meal times. Younger children can stir dishes and help set the table. Older ones can plan and cook a complete meal.

Have a new babysitter visit and play
with the children several times before
being left alone with them.

Take time to play and relax.
Everyone needs downtime—even children.

A baby's nails grow quickly and can cause deep scratches. The best time to trim them is after bath time when little nails are soft and your baby is mellow.

Children need schedules and routine.
They need things to be in order and to know
ahead of time what is going to happen. It helps
them feel loved and secure in a crazy world.

Don't worry if your teen seems to have a negative reaction toward the opposite sex. Some teens are late bloomers.

Show love and respect for your children even when you are angry. Criticize your child's problem behavior, not your child.

Set limits. Catering to your children's every whim only creates spoiled children.

February 10

Limit TV and video game time. Excessive hours in these areas mean lack of exercise, which can lead to future health problems.

When teaching preschoolers to dress themselves, roll up complete outfits together. They can then pull out the day's clothes easily.

Be prepared to answer lots of questions.
But ask some yourself. Encourage children
to think about the "why" behind things.

Invite a lonely family over for Thanksgiving dinner or take dinner to a needy family. Face-to-face giving is the kind that will make an impression on your children.

February 12

Take your family to church. Worship and prayer are an important part of healthy, loving families.

As long as your baby is fed, dry, and clothed properly, a little fussing is okay.

Children who spend time around people
of all ages are better prepared socially.
Provide opportunities for them to interact
with a variety of different age levels.

Teaching basic skills like counting is easy and fun. Use everyday situations like setting the table to count, learn colors, and practice names.

Give your children Valentines.
Dads, bring home flowers for your daughters.
Moms, buy some candy for your sons.

For great family laughs, have a story-telling circle. Have someone start the story, then at some point stop that person mid-sentence. The next person picks up the story from there. This hilarious exercise teaches children to think on their feet and promotes creativity and logical thought.

Learn to listen. Your children will talk
to you if they know you are going to take
the time to hear them out.

Warm baths soothe and relax fussy babies.

I have no greater joy than to hear
that my children walk in truth.

3 JOHN 1:4

Buy clothes on clearance for the next year.
Buy one size ahead of what
your child wears now.

Don't be afraid to set limits.
Children not only need them, they want them.
(No matter what they tell you.)

If it seem evil unto you to serve the LORD, choose
you this day whom ye will serve. . .but as for me
and my house, we will serve the LORD.

JOSHUA 24:15

Pray for your children every day.
They need the prayers, and you need
the quiet time alone with God.

Make a monthly menu, repeating simple, favorite meals on the same day each week.

No matter how old your children are, they are still your children. Don't expect to quit worrying about them when they leave home.

If some of your children tend to be worriers, encourage them to come up with solutions—on paper. This takes the focus off the negative and helps them develop problem-solving skills.

Let your children do things on their own.
You can supervise if necessary, but letting them
dress themselves or shop for their own clothes
fosters independence and responsibility.

Mark all the pieces to a puzzle on the back with the same number. When your preschooler dumps them all together, sorting through them will be much easier.

Persistence is a wonderful character quality. Make children finish what they start and help them to hang in there when things are tough.

Traditions are an excellent way to bring families closer. Come up with some that are special to your family, and you will probably see your children honoring those traditions with their own children one day.

Never argue with your spouse in front of the children. It confuses and upsets younger ones and sets a poor example for the older ones.

Keep games and puzzles organized on shelves.
Remove game pieces from boxes and
put them into zippered plastic bags to
keep them from getting lost.

Make your home a safe harbor for your children—a place where they can be themselves and know they are loved, a place of protection from the world.

Do something wacky and totally
out of the ordinary. Your children
will talk about it for years.

Beat the bedtime battle by setting a regular time for your children to go to bed. Allow reading time or provide a favorite toy—anything that establishes good nighttime habits.

November 8

Watch the news with your children and talk about it together. This strategy can promote a balanced worldview while relieving your child's anxiety about what's happening in the world.

February 25

Catch your children being good!
Rewarding good behavior when it happens is
a great way to reinforce positive attributes.

Prejudice is learned at home—enough said.

When bringing a new baby home, prepare small gifts for the siblings. Presents will be flowing freely for the new addition, and this will keep the others from feeling left out.

Trace your family heritage and roots. Cultural inheritances can be a wonderful way to bond as a family.

Encourage your children to share their things and cooperate with others. These are necessary skills that will serve them well as adults.

Words to say daily: "I'm glad you're my child."
Let them know why you think
they're special—often.

February 28

Homemade birthday parties are often the best! Keep things simple. Invite a few friends, have a sleepover, and use disposable dishes.

November 4

Spend the day serving the homeless as a family. Your children will learn to appreciate the things they might otherwise take for granted.

Jesus said, "Verily I say unto you, Except ye be converted, and become as little children, ye shall not enter into the kingdom of heaven."

MATTHEW 18:3

Share "just because" gifts with your family. These should be little gifts that you give them just because you love them.

Start putting toddlers on the potty chair
as soon as they can walk. By the time
they are ready to be trained, the potty chair
will be familiar and comfortable.

Make a Thankful Tree. Have each family member cut out two or more paper leaves and decorate them with what they are thankful for.

Pre-teens should be allowed to solve some of their own problems. Giving them all the answers or keeping them from the consequences of their mistakes will take away their opportunity to grow in skill and character.

November 1

Even a child is known by his doings, whether his work be pure, and whether it be right.

PROVERBS 20:11

Words to say daily: "How can I help you?"
Your children need to know
you're there for them.

Dress children appropriately for the weather.
Put on layers that can be removed
if it warms up outside.

Organized sports are a great way
to teach children discipline and
provide daily exercise. They also foster
team spirit and good sportsmanship.

A great way to schedule family time is a weekend brunch. Hold a special "let's get together" time on Saturday or Sunday. Invite extended family.

Encourage your children to express
their feelings in a proper manner and setting.
Learning to deal with feelings ahead
of time helps avoid problems later.

Let your children see you reading your Bible and spending time in prayer. If God is important to you, He will be important to them, as well.

When introducing solid food to infants,
give them vegetables before fruits.
They will learn to love them immediately.

Don't interrupt when your children
are talking to you. Let them express their
thoughts before you share yours.

Encourage creativity by exposing your children to music, dance, the arts, and other activities that help them to develop their imaginations.

October 27

Tell your children the story of their births. Children love to hear about the day they were born and how special they are to you.

While quality time is nice in theory,
it doesn't make up for quantity—both
are vitally important.

Trust your children, but don't put them into the path of temptation. Even the best child can get into trouble if left unsupervised at the wrong time and place.

Avoid giving children drinks after 7:00 p.m.
This will help prevent bed-wetting.

Support your child's teacher.
Take any calls or notes sent home seriously.
If your child misbehaves at school,
reinforce the discipline at home.

Whatever the situation, clearly outline the rules.
Children need to know what
is expected of them.

To avoid the risk of being kidnapped,
tell children to scream as loud as they
can if someone tries to take them away.

Safety Tip: Limit visitors and trips out with new babies. The fewer people the new baby is exposed to, the less the chance of illness.

Limit commitments that take
you away from your family.
Your children won't be with you forever.

Keeping fresh, healthy on-the-go snacks and drinks—such as carrot sticks and bottled water—available to carry in the car will help you avoid costly fast food stops.

Teach children to do their own laundry.
Start by helping younger ones with the goal of
preparing them to fly solo by the age of ten.
Each child should have an assigned laundry day.

March 14

Empathy means understanding how others feel. Showing your children how to empathize with others will help them avoid becoming self-centered.

Safety Tip: Keep a well-stocked first
aid kit in the car. Double up on Band-Aids.
Toddlers love them for boo-boos.

Safety Tip: Take one afternoon and do a walk-through of your home. Look for hazards such as long cords, medicines, and cleaning supplies or electrical outlets without covers that are within a child's reach.

Prepare well-balanced, nutritious meals
for your children, but don't stop there.
Teach them the basics of a healthy diet—they'll
be feeding themselves one day.

Talk to your children. Begin while they are in the womb. Babies love to listen to their parents' voices.

Don't feel threatened when your children challenge your authority. See it as an opportunity to teach them the purpose behind discipline and guidelines.

Find something to praise each of
your children for daily. It will provide a
much-needed boost to their self-esteem.

Show your children whom to approach
if they need help from a stranger.
Policemen, store clerks, and mothers
with children are good choices.

Who is a wise man and endued with knowledge among you? let him shew out of a good conversation his works with meekness of wisdom.

JAMES 3:13

Preview videos and video games before letting your children watch them. Industry ratings are good, but parental ratings are better.

Safety Tip: Never put a baby to
bed with a bottle. It can lead to serious
tooth decay and may cause choking.

Before I formed thee in the belly I knew thee;
and before thou camest forth out
of the womb I sanctified thee.

JEREMIAH 1:5

To keep up with your children's homework requirements, designate a particular time and place to complete the day's work.

Color-coded towels and linens are a great way to help children learn to take care of their personal area. You'll know exactly who left his or her towel on the bathroom floor or linens in the dryer.

Always carry an extra change of clothes for children when going on daylong outings. This holds true for older children, as well.

Safety Tip: Know where your children are at all times and establish mandatory check-in times even when they are playing in your yard.

Safety Tip: Establish an escape route in case of a fire, and designate a place for everyone to meet in the event of an emergency evacuation.

One of the most important things you can give your children is time. Be sure to spend time with them every day.

Perk up hand-me-down clothing by adding new trim, buttons, or hemlines. Patches and fabric paint can be used to turn something old into something new.

Limit your children's after-school involvement to one activity. Children can burn out, too.

Requiring your children to say "Please" and "Thank you" promotes a sense of thankfulness and encourages an appreciation for manners.

Safety Tip: Teach your youngest children your full names. "Mommy" and "Daddy" won't help if they are lost.

Children love to pretend. Keep a box with dress-up supplies handy, and stock it with shoes, gloves, and hats from a thrift store.

Children—girls and boys—love to sew.
Provide needles, fabric, and scissors and wait
to see who gets excited about the project.

Be a letter writer and encourage your children to write them, as well. Letters are a wonderful way to communicate and an appreciated gesture. They also make great keepsakes.

Buy identical socks for each of your children.
Then there is no need to worry
about mismatched socks.

Be loving and affectionate in front of the children. It allows them to see how much Mom and Dad mean to each other.

If your child has problems hearing or talking, it could be from chronic ear infections. Have his or her ears checked out immediately.

Keep a journal of the funny things your children say. You may think you'll remember them—but odds are you won't.

Both parents need to be involved in their children's lives. Dad and Mom are equally important in a child's development.

Boys need to be boys. Wrestle and play
rough with them. They will love it!

Before allowing your children to talk you into bringing home a pet, carefully consider the ages of your children, the amount of care the pet will require, and the size of your home.

Choose at least one night out of the month
and make dinner something special.
Get out the good china and dress up.
Believe it or not, your children will soon
look forward to these refined evening events.

October 5

Hold family conferences to decide issues that affect everyone. While you still have the ultimate say-so on the matter, your children will learn that you value their opinions and ideas.

Safety Tip: Never leave a baby unattended
on a changing table or bed.

Words to say daily: "I love you."
Three very powerful little words.

Jesus said, Suffer little children,
and forbid them not, to come unto me:
for of such is the kingdom of heaven.

MATTHEW 19:14

If you want grateful children, express gratefulness yourself. Thank them for completing chores or helping around the house.

April 2

Encourage environmental responsibility.
Recycle as a family. Make your home
as energy efficient as possible.

Help your children dream about what they might be when they grow up. Point out their talents and traits and suggest careers that would match.

Words to say daily: "How about a hug?"
Even teens need hugs.

Casting all your care upon him;
for he careth for you.

1 PETER 5:7

Celebrate religious holidays together.
Faith makes strong families.

September 30

Safety Tip: Remove rubber tips from doorstoppers. It won't change their effectiveness and will eliminate a choking hazard for your small children.

A designated "time-out" spot works best for children three to six years of age. Younger children won't understand the concept.

Let your children see you standing up for what's right. They will draw courage from your courage.

Require children to pick up after themselves at a very young age—even toddlers can put their toys away.

Safety Tip: Keep photo identification
of your children with you at all times.

Safety Tip: If your bedrooms are on second or third floors, place fire escape ladders in each room.

Foster a good work ethic in your children.
Don't worry—a little hard work
won't hurt them.

Children learn through play. Provide them with toys that foster fun and promote learning.

If you say no, mean it.
Don't give in to whining or manipulation.
Your children will learn to
distrust your judgment.

Plant a garden. Growing and harvesting food teaches children to appreciate every meal.

Remember that discipline has to do with right and wrong, appropriate and inappropriate behavior—not with the emotional condition of the parent.

Get involved in your community. Plant trees,
pick up trash, and help your neighbors.
Demonstrate for your children how
to be responsible citizens.

Safety Tip: Insist that your children check in with you before leaving home for any reason—even for a few minutes.

April 11

Your child's first visit to the dentist should occur by the age of three with regular checkups to follow.

Give your children a choice about a certain activity or event only if it really is optional. If it is mandatory, simply be up front about it.

Don't hesitate to unexpectedly drop in on or check up on your children. It provides an additional incentive for them to make good choices, and it shows that you care.

Be reliable. If you say you'll pick your children up at a certain time—be there.

Help your children deal with the loss of a loved one by suggesting that you create a memory collage together. A poster or scrapbook full of pictures, thoughts, and other treasures keeps that person alive in their hearts.

Time-outs are good for parents, too.
Before dealing with a situation, take a deep
breath, walk out of the room, and count to ten.
You will be able to react more calmly.

Go for walks as a family. It's a fun and healthy way to relax and spend time together.

Write letters to your children, starting as early as possible. Present them to your children when they're grown as a very special gift.

April 15

The heart of the wise teacheth his mouth,
and addeth learning to his lips.

PROVERBS 16:23

Use decorative doorknob covers to prevent toddlers from opening doors and slipping out.

April 16

Scheduled play dates are a great way
for parents and young children
to ensure time for having fun.

If you cannot be there when your children arrive home from school, enroll them in an after-school program or arrange for a trusted friend or family member to be present.

Safety Tip: Take a family class on CPR and first aid to ensure you're prepared for emergencies.

Monitor your children to keep
them out of trouble. Ask the four Ws:
who, what, when, and where.

Talk with your children about sex in a way that is appropriate for their ages. Young children only want a simple answer. Don't overload them with unnecessary information.

Provide babysitters with a list
of rules for your children. It's risky
to expect the sitter to guess at the rules
or depend on the children to fill in the blanks.

Hug your children and be physically affectionate
with them. Especially for girls, receiving
affection at home will make them
less likely to seek it elsewhere.

A new commandment I give unto you,
That ye love one another; as I have loved you,
that ye also love one another.

JOHN 13:34

You can only do so much to properly train your children. Don't sweat the small stuff.

Get to know your children's friends and their families. Be aware of their values and family situations.

Don't push your goals and dreams
onto your children. Encourage them
to develop their own dreams.

Children need sleep (and lots of it!) to grow properly. Establish a regular bedtime and make sure they get eight to ten hours of sleep daily.

Praise children for trying hard, no matter what the outcome. Winning really isn't everything.

Touch your children often. Something as simple as patting their shoulder as they walk by says, "I love you."

Seek to be a parent to your children rather than a friend. Your children will have lots of friends, but only you can fill the critical role of parent in their lives.

September 11

Spending one-on-one time with each of your children is a good way to avoid sibling rivalry.

Require your teens to practice basic hygiene. Daily baths, properly brushed teeth, and freshly washed hair never hurt anyone.

September 10

Don't lie—such as instructing your children
to say you aren't home to unwelcome callers.
Don't steal—such as failing to mention too
much change given back to you at the store.
Don't cheat—such as returning merchandise
you or your children have damaged.
If your children see you do these things,
they'll follow your example.

April 25

Visit a nursing home and take your children
with you. Bring along flowers or small gifts
and encourage your children to visit with
the residents. You may be surprised to
see who enjoys themselves the most.

Between the ages of ten and thirteen, children change almost overnight. The need for privacy changes, and they are often more sensitive. Be ready to make necessary adjustments.

Your children won't fully appreciate owning a car until they are able to cover the costs of maintenance and upkeep.

Don't embarrass your children by yelling at officials when you attend sporting events.

Educate yourself about learning disabilities and watch your children for signs. Early diagnosis and treatment can help your child avoid years of frustration and damage to self-esteem.

Teach your children not to be afraid to stand alone. Learning to deal with peer pressure will help them avoid poor choices.

Choose your battles with your teens carefully.
It makes no sense to win the
battle if you lose the war.

Encourage your children to develop good conversation skills by engaging each child in conversation for a few minutes each day.

Send your children outside to play.
Everyone needs fresh air and sunlight.

When baby-proofing your home,
crawl around the floor. You will get a
look from a baby's point of view.

Make May Day baskets and share them with your neighbors. This will help your children learn to extend themselves to others.

Words to say daily: "How was your day?"
Then listen to what your children have to say.

Her children arise up, and call her blessed;
her husband also, and he praiseth her.

PROVERBS 31:28

Being a parent is the most important
work you'll ever do. Take it seriously,
but don't forget to enjoy every moment.

Read to your children regularly. It is a great way to spend time together while teaching them to love the written word.

If homework becomes an issue with one of your children, ask the teacher to send home a note with your child each day verifying receipt of assignments from the day before and confirming new assignments.

Partner with God. Prayer is the most powerful weapon you can employ on behalf of your children.

Children's children are the crown of old men;
and the glory of children are their fathers.

PROVERBS 17:6

Words to say daily: "Please."
Manners shouldn't be limited to children.

Teach your children how and when to thoroughly wash their hands. This is the first major defense in avoiding illness.

When relatives or friends disagree with you
concerning how to handle your children,
stay calm, stand firm, and never discuss
it in front of your children.

Schedule an appointment with your children's
teachers before the school year begins.
Offer to become an active partner
in a successful school year.

May 6

Require your children to write thank you
notes. This one small task inspires gratitude,
encourages a respect for etiquette,
and teaches important letter-writing skills.

Make your house the after-school hangout. Provide snacks and a place for your children and their friends to relax. You won't have to wonder where they are or what they are doing.

When to talk to your children about "the birds and the bees" will depend on their age and maturity level. Handle with prayer.

Breaking a promise or failing to keep your word can deeply affect your children. If you aren't prepared to deliver, don't promise.

May 8

Require your children to show respect for their elders. You will be teaching them to cherish life and the wisdom it brings.

Self-defense classes for children build independence, security, and self-esteem. Consider enrolling your child in one today.

If your children refuse to pick up their things, confiscate them and require your children to "buy" them back with additional chores.

Prepare your children for kindergarten and let them feel your enthusiasm. Pay a visit to the school together ahead of time, and buy a new outfit or backpack to make the first day special.

May 10

All little girls need a doll to love and take care of, preparing them for the wonders of motherhood.

In regard to toys, less is most often more.
Keep a variety of toys on hand—books, blocks,
dolls, toy cars, puzzles—but avoid clutter.
Too many options can actually create
restlessness and anxiety.

Safety Tip: As warm weather approaches,
enroll your children in a local swimming class
that also teaches good water safety skills.
You could be saving their lives.

Safety Tip: Children should always wear a helmet
and reflective clothing when riding a bike.

To keep the toy box from overflowing,
have your children surrender a toy
whenever they wish to buy a new one.

Regular eye checkups for your children
can prevent the onset of headaches
and poor performance at school.

Do not let a child who has a physical
or mental handicap rule the family.
Such children will benefit from firm
guidelines as much as their siblings.

When shopping for back-to-school
supplies, check local sales flyers.
Then, if possible, shop at the store that
offers to honor other store's sale prices.

Set realistic goals for your children.
Left unchallenged, they will become bored;
pushed too hard, they will
become frustrated and resentful.

August 21

If it becomes necessary to spend time away
from home with an infant, take the
playpen along with you put your little
one in a playpen for naps. Your baby will
sleep soundly in familiar surroundings.

May 15

A woman when she is in travail hath sorrow,
because her hour is come: but as soon as
she is delivered of the child,
she remembereth no more the anguish,
for joy that a man is born into the world.

JOHN 16:21

Teach your children—boys *and girls*—how to handle routine car maintenance tasks.

Practice memorizing scripture together.
Children as young as two can
memorize simple Bible verses.

Safety Tip: Password-protect your computer. Children should never have access to the Internet while unattended.

Respectful children are a blessing. Teach your children to address adults in respectful terms.

Help your children set priorities
by answering questions such as
"What do I need to accomplish today?" and
"What do I need to do for others today?"

Practice good table manners at home, even when your children are little. Taking them out to eat will be a pleasure rather than an embarrassment.

Limit the amount of hours your teenager can work. Although it is good training for the future, too much work can interfere with school.

Allow access to arts and crafts material to foster creativity. Paints, glue, construction paper, and crayons can provide hours of entertainment.

August 16

When sending your student off to college, pack a suitcase full of basics with things like sheets, towel and washcloth sets, an iron, and change for the Laundromat.

The more children experience, the more they learn about their world. Provide new experiences when you can. Go for walks and visit museums and zoos. The opportunities are limitless if you're looking for them.

August 15

A merry heart doeth good like a medicine:
but a broken spirit drieth the bones.

PROVERBS 17:22

Laugh a lot! Laughter is good medicine and an important coping tool—especially during tough times.

Educate your teens about the pros and cons of credit. Odds are they will begin to receive credit card offers even before they leave home.

Talk to your children about societal dangers like drugs, alcohol, and smoking. Do it early, do it often, and set a good example.

Nagging will do nothing but drive your children in the wrong direction. Make your expectations clear and then greet noncompliance with appropriate consequences.

When checking into day care for your children,
look for accredited quality child care
homes with a low adult-to-child ratio.

Allow your children to grow their own plants—even if you live in an apartment. Plants, even in pots, teach responsibility and resource management. You may even discover a blossoming "green thumb."

May 24

See that your children receive regular physical checkups. Early detection of medical problems can greatly increase treatment options.

Praise, praise, praise! Children need positive reinforcement daily.

Digital cameras are fantastic tools for making memories. Consider investing in one and use it often.

Hold your children responsible for their actions by allowing them to deal with the consequences of poor choices. The exception would be when the consequences further expose them to danger.

To get a fussy baby to sleep, buckle your little one into a car seat and sit it on top of a dryer that is running. The calm noise and quiet motion will put them right to sleep.

August 9

Teach your children to deal with reality. Sadness, hurt, and pain are all part of life. You will help you children by refusing to pretend otherwise.

Toddlers learn by repetition. Be willing to read the same book over and over and practice the same words and skills with them daily.

Share your passions with your children.
Let them know they can make a difference
in the world around them.

Houseplants add beauty and warmth to any home, but some can pose a danger for your small children. Do your homework and choose wisely.

Words to say daily: "Let's all work together."
Being a family is a team effort.

Keep plenty of snacks on hand. Teenagers can
wipe out a kitchen before you know it.

Keep preschoolers entertained for hours by letting them "wash" dishes at the sink. Pull up a chair, prepare a few inches of bubble water, and let your little one wash plastic plates and cups.

Teach your children the meaning of all the holidays. For example, they should know Memorial Day honors the sacrifices of those who fought and died for our freedom.

Set your children up for success by encouraging them to pursue challenging opportunities. An "I can" attitude is best learned by experience.

Rocking chairs are great for babies. Parents often find them restful and comforting, as well.

Of all nature's gifts to the human race,
what is sweeter to a man than his children?

CICERO

The just man walketh in his integrity:
his children are blessed after him.

PROVERBS 20:7

A central command center is great for families with busy schedules. Create a place to post notes, write messages, and keep calendars up-to-date. An area in the kitchen often works best.

June 2

Safety Tip: Make sure your children drink lots of water during the summer. Dehydration is a silent danger.

Reversing letters when writing can be normal for a child learning to read. But if complete words and sentences are reversed on a regular basis, it could be a sign of dyslexia.

Create white noise to help children sleep. Play soothing music or run a fan in the background to help drown out distracting noises.

Provoke not your children to wrath:
but bring them up in the nurture
and admonition of the Lord.

EPHESIANS 6:4

June 4

Words to say daily: "You can do it."
Children thrive on encouragement.

Model proper ways to be affectionate with others—showing is better than telling.

June 5

Protect your children from sexual abuse by teaching them what is and isn't appropriate touching. Teach them that they can and should say no and then tell you immediately.

Good citizenship is best taught by example.
Get your family involved in your
community—vote and volunteer.

Encourage your children to honor
Father's Day and Mother's Day.
Help them with ideas and execution,
but avoid the temptation to do it all for them.

Stay connected to your children
by talking to them daily. Don't wait
for a crisis to get caught up.

June 7

Safety Tip: A child's skin is especially sensitive and vulnerable to sun damage. Insist on the use of sunscreen and hats, and avoid exposure to the sun during the hottest part of the day.

You have a tremendous influence over
your children's senses of self-worth.
Work consistently to help your
children believe in themselves.

It really is okay to have pancakes and ice cream for dinner—occasionally!

Don't try to give your children everything.
It isn't in your child's best interest.
It leaves your children with selfish
and unrealistic expectations.

Safety Tip: Keep activated charcoal and syrup of ipecac on hand in case of poisoning. The charcoal helps absorb some poisons and ipecac induces vomiting. Post the Poison Control Center number near the phone.

No matter how short the drive, always buckle up your children in the car. Most car accidents involving children occur within twenty minutes of the home.

Be firm when you need to leave one of your children in the nursery or with a sitter. Hug them, explain that you will be back to get them, and leave. Lingering sends your child a mixed signal and will increase anxiety.

Expect your children to accept responsibility. Doing for them what they can do for themselves inhibits maturity and independence.

Can't afford a big family vacation? Take mini vacations close to home. Day trips can provide a great deal of fun and a much-needed break.

Love your children unconditionally. Let them know you may dislike their behavior or action, but you will always love them.

Have family devotions every evening with your
children. Establishing time for God
each evening is the most important
principle you can instill in your children.

When you're unsure of the proper response or attitude you should have in order to raise your child God's way, just ask yourself, "What would Jesus do?" and you won't go wrong!

Introduce your children to the great outdoors
early in life. It will awaken their senses
and give them an appreciation for
God's magnificent creation.

Safety Tip: Teach your children what information should not be given to strangers who call on the phone.

Little deeds of kindness.
Little words of love.
Help to make earth happy,
Like the Heaven above!

Julia Fletcher Carney

Provide opportunities for your children to build warm, deep attachments to family and close family friends. Family ties provide security and a sense of identity.

June 15

When going on long car trips with children,
pack backpacks with "boredom busters."
Crayons, coloring books, small toys,
and hand-held games are all great choices.

Be aware of sudden changes in your child's behavior or physical appearance. A smart, well-informed parent is an effective parent.

June 16

He that handleth a matter wisely shall find good:
and whoso trusteth in the LORD, happy is he.

PROVERBS 16:20

Keep a supply of bubbles in the car for a distraction when you're stuck in traffic.

June 17

Classical music stimulates the brain and soothes the soul. Expose your children to it early and often.

In the battle for a clean room, establish specific guidelines. A place for everything and everything in its place, beds made properly, no leftover food or drink, and clothing treated with care.

When your children start to make
you feel like your back is against the wall,
take a few moments to pray and regroup.
You will all be better off for it.

Be consistent and fair when enforcing rules with teenagers. Make sure they understand your expectations and the consequences of disregarding them.

June 19

Moms: Be kind and loving to your sons,
but resist the temptation to coddle them.
Learning to accept responsibility is a
necessary preparation for manhood.

Teach your children—boys and girls—
basic household skills and yard care.

Insist that your children dress appropriately for the situation. This teaches respect for others and promotes a favorable self-image.

A soft answer turneth away wrath:
but grievous words stir up anger.

PROVERBS 15:1

Sacred and happy homes are the surest
guarantees for the moral progress of a nation.

HENRY DRUMMOND

When traveling with babies or toddlers, pack a
backpack or pillowcase with a favorite blanket
and a few favorite toys from home.
When you stop for breaks, look for a place
to spread out the blanket and let them crawl
around. Babies need to stretch their legs, too.

June 22

The best way to teach your children
modesty is to be modest even at home.

If you introduce vegetables early, most children will naturally love them. But if that doesn't work, try pureeing or grating the vegetables and adding them to soups, meatloaf, or stews.

If your children are old enough to play board games, they are old enough to play by the rules and graciously accept a win or a loss.
Resist the urge to throw the game in their favor.

Start training your teens early for the
day they will live on their own.
Talk about budgeting, cooking, and
independent living while they are still at home.

June 24

Your children will sometimes feel
they are in the boxing ring of life.
Let them know you are in their corner.

Talk with your teens often about their friends. Don't assume they will make wise choices without input and encouragement.

Hug your children often.
It's a small gesture with a great return.

If you want your children to write while they are away, place pre-addressed, stamped postcards and envelopes in their luggage.

End TV, video games, and computer
time at least one hour before bedtime.
Children need time to settle down their
brain activity before they can sleep well.

A well-behaved child is the result of good parental training rather than luck.

Safety Tip: To prevent the spread of illness,
teach children to cough or
sneeze into the crook of the arm.

Words to say daily: "You did a great job."
Children need to be appreciated.

Encourage your "late bloomer" or
"early bloomer" with the assurance
that people mature at different rates,
but everyone gets there eventually.

July 7

Encourage your children to look forward to tomorrow by asking each child to share a reason to bounce out of bed the next morning.

Introduce your children to photography and get a glimpse of how they view the world.

July 6

Children will entertain themselves with whatever is available for play. Encourage these early expressions of ingenuity and creativity.

Celebrate rather than judge
your children's creative efforts.
They need appreciation not criticism.

Where can one better be than in
the bosom of one's family?

AUTHOR UNKNOWN